JUN - - 2006

P9-ARA-391

The Library of SPIDERS™

Daddy Longlegs Spiders

JAKE MILLER

The Rosen Publishing Group's
PowerKids Press™

3 1267 13885 8830

Published in 2004 by The Rosen Publishing Group, Inc.
29 East 21st Street, New York, NY 10010

Copyright © 2004 by The Rosen Publishing Group, Inc.

All rights reserved. No part of this book may be reproduced in any form without permission in writing from the publisher, except by a reviewer.

First Edition

Editor: Jannell Khu
Book Design: Emily Muschinske

Photo Credits: Cover, pp. 3, 5, 6, 9 (top left), 13, 17, 18, 22 © Ed Nieuwenhuys; pp. 7, 9 (top right, bottom left and right), 14 © Wim Van Egmond; p. 10 © James Rowan; p. 11 © Robert & Linda Mitchel, p. 13 (inset) © Malcolm Storey, p. 21 © David Liebman; p. 21 (inset) © Corbis.

Miller, Jake, 1969–
Daddy longlegs spiders / Jake Miller.
    p. cm. — (The library of spiders)
Summary: Describes the anatomy, web-making, food, reproduction, enemies, and usefulness to humans of the Daddy longleg spider, which is often confused with other longlegged insects, and mistakenly feared as poisonous.
Includes bibliographical references (p.   ).
ISBN 0-8239-6706-9 (lib. bdg.)
1. Pholcidae—Juvenile literature. [1. Daddy longleg spiders. 2. Spiders.] I. Title. II. Series.
QL458.42.P4 M55 2004
595.4'3—dc21

2002010544

Manufactured in the United States of America

Contents

The Daddy Longlegs Spider

Spider Bites

The daddy longlegs spider gained its name because it has legs that can be from 5 to 20 times as long as its body. If this were the same for people, an average person might have legs that were from 15 to 60 feet (4.5–18 m) long!

No matter where you are, there's a pretty good chance that there is a daddy longlegs spider nearby. They are called daddy longlegs spiders because they have very long, thin legs. They are sometimes called cellar spiders, because they like to live in basements. They also live in houses and barns. Some like to live in caves, in spaces between rocks, and in piles of leaves on the ground. Most kinds of daddy longlegs spiders live in the **tropics**, where it is warm. However, these spiders are also happy to live in places where it is cold outside, as long as they are inside a nice, warm house.

Daddy longlegs are commonly found in cellars, caves, and other sheltered places where there might be a lot of yummy bugs to eat.

These spiders are different kinds of Pholcidae. Notice that the spiders all have long, thin legs. The front legs of daddy longlegs spiders are especially long.

Pholcidae

Daddy longlegs spiders belong to a group, or family, of spiders that scientists call **Pholcidae**. There are more than 300 **species** of Pholcidae. *Pholcus phalangioides* is the scientific name for one of the most common species, or kinds, of daddy longlegs spider. Most spiders live alone, but there are a few species of Pholcidae that live together on the same web. They usually share their food, but sometimes they fight with, and even eat, each other!

One way that scientists can tell different kinds of spiders apart is to count the spiders' eyes. Most daddy longlegs spiders have eight eyes. They have two sets of three eyes on each side of the head and two smaller eyes in the middle. However, some daddy longlegs only have six eyes.

This is a photo of a daddy longlegs spider's face. Can you see its eight eyes? There are three eyes on the left and right sides of its face. It also has two smaller eyes in the middle.

The Daddy Longlegs Spider's Body

Daddy longlegs spiders are **arachnids**. Arachnids have four pairs of legs and two body parts. The head is called the **cephalothorax**. Daddy longlegs spiders have round heads. The back part of a spider's body is called the **abdomen**. It is hot dog–shaped and usually measures between ⅛ and ⅝ inch (.3–1.5 cm) long. The bodies of daddy longlegs spiders can be gray, brown, or green. Their pale, thin legs are about 2 inches (5 cm) long.

(Top) Notice the differences between the harvestman pictured on the right and the daddy longlegs spider on the left.

(Bottom) This picture shows the daddy longlegs spider's cephalothorax, abdomen, fangs, and legs. Pedipalps are the second pair of legs on arachnids. Daddy longlegs spiders have thin, pale legs except for the dark joint where the legs bend.

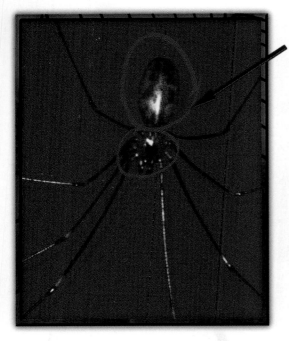

(Left) Daddy longlegs spiders clearly have two body parts, the cephalothorax and the abdomen.

(Right) The harvestman is also known as daddy longlegs. However, the harvestman differs from all true spiders because its body is not divided in two separate parts.

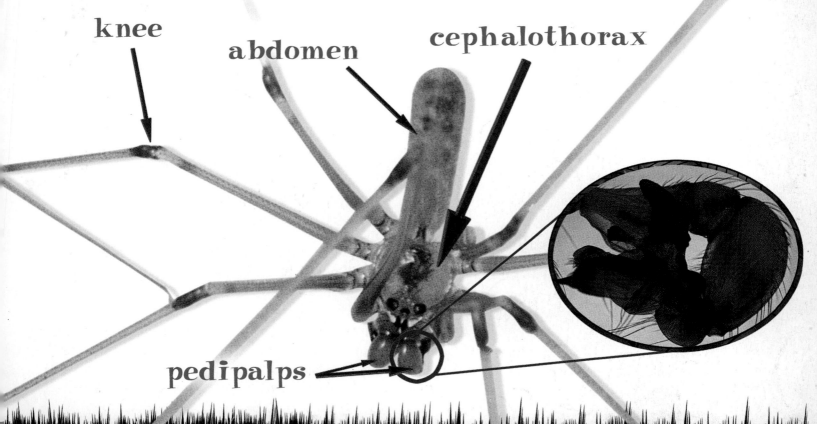

knee

abdomen

cephalothorax

pedipalps

The long, thin legs of daddy longlegs spiders help them to blend into their web. Their legs look like strands of the web. This makes it very difficult for their prey and their enemies to see daddy longlegs spiders.

Long Legs in Action

The long, thin legs of a daddy longlegs spider are not as strong as some other spiders' legs. However, their legs help the daddy longlegs spiders to **survive**. Their legs are so pale and thin that they look like part of a web. This makes it very hard to spot a daddy longlegs spider. By the time the **unsuspecting prey** walk or fly into the daddy longlegs spider's web, it is too late for them.

Daddy longlegs spiders use their legs to help them feel things that are far away from their body. For instance, the daddy longlegs spider's legs help it to sense an approaching enemy before the enemy is close enough to attack. The long legs also help the spider to move very quickly in its web, either to catch prey or to run away from an enemy.

One of the
smallest
Pholcidae in the
world is *Ninetis
subtilissima*,
which comes
from a small
Middle Eastern
country called
Yemen. Its body
is only .04 inch
(1 mm) long.

A Messy Web

Some spiders build **complicated** webs that look beautiful. Daddy longlegs spiders' webs are tangled and messy. The webs are not sticky, but there are so many strings that an insect that flies into a web gets confused. The daddy longlegs spider can feel that something has hit its web. Before the insect can find its way out of the web, the daddy longlegs spider attacks. As do all spiders, the daddy longlegs spider spins string for its web with its silk **glands**. The daddy longlegs spider has four **spinnerets** at the back of its abdomen, from where the silk flows.

Daddy longlegs spiders spin messy webs as a way to trap their prey. Daddy longlegs spiders spin their webs in dark corners and other out-of-sight places.

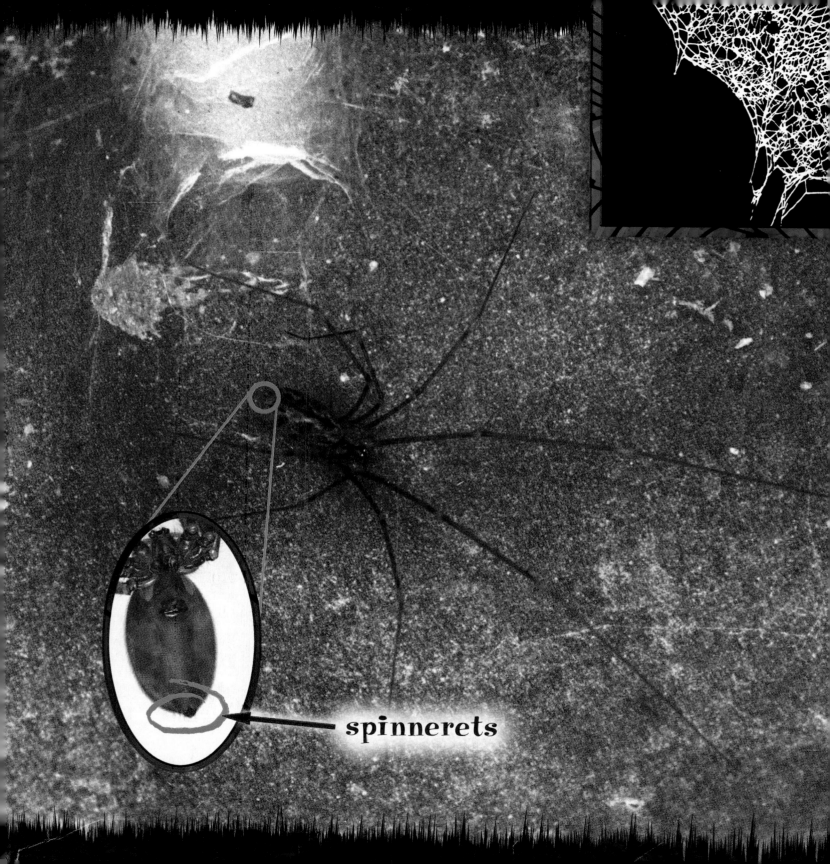

spinnerets

Patience has finally paid off. An insect is caught and becomes a tasty meal for this daddy longlegs spider.

Hunting for Food

Daddy longlegs spiders spend most of their time hanging upside down from the bottom of their webs. They stay very still and wait for prey to get caught in their webs. They eat many kinds of insects, such as flies, mosquitoes, moths, and beetles. They even eat other spiders. When a daddy longlegs spider attacks, it moves very quickly. It spins silk to wrap around the prey. Then the daddy longlegs spider bites its prey. The **venom** in its bite **paralyzes** the prey. After the venom turns the inside of the prey's body into liquid, the daddy longlegs spider sucks the liquid out of the body.

Daddy longlegs spiders will eat almost any insects, including beetles and mosquitoes. The spider uses its fangs to bite the insect once it is wrapped up. Venom from the fangs will turn the prey's insides into liquid, which the spider sucks up.

Laying Eggs

A male daddy longlegs spider begins to search for a mate when he is about one year old. He leaves his web and wanders until he finds a female who is ready to **breed**. When he finds a female, he shakes her web in a special way to show that he is looking for a mate. If he shakes the web incorrectly, the female might think he is prey and eat him. After mating, the female daddy longlegs spider lays from 15 to 30 eggs. When she hunts outside her web, she attaches the eggs to her web for safekeeping.

After laying her eggs, the female daddy longlegs spider wraps the eggs in a few strands of silk and carries the bundle around in her mouth.

Sometimes if a male finds a female who is not yet old enough to mate, the male waits until she gets older. A male lives for only a year. He mates and then dies. A female lives for up to three years and can mate many times.

Baby Daddy Longlegs Spiders

From two to three weeks after the female lays her eggs, they begin to hatch. The baby daddy longlegs spiders are so pale that they are almost **transparent** when they are born. They are born with short legs. They don't look like daddy longlegs spiders yet!

The mother is careful to protect them from other spiders and from insects that want to eat them. However, if some of the babies are slow to hatch, the mother or the other baby spiders eat them. The babies stay with their mother for about nine days. They eat the yolk from their eggs, and they practice hunting. When they have grown a little, they shed their skin and wander off to find a corner where they can spin a web of their own.

When the eggs are ready to hatch, the female spider hangs the egg bundle on a web. The baby spiders are transparent and have short legs until they shed their skin for the first time. During the time the babies remain with their mother, she carries the young spiders around in her jaws as shown in this picture.

Daddy longlegs spiders shed their skin when they grow. This is called molting. They shed nine times before they are fully grown. They need to shed their skin because the outer layer of their skin is hard and cannot stretch as they grow.

Defensive Dancer

If something too big for the daddy longlegs spider to eat bumps into its web, the spider does a weird dance. It may whirl or shake its body. Sometimes it looks as if it is doing push-ups as fast as it can. If it shakes fast enough, it turns into a blur and can be hard for enemies to see. The shaking might also help to shake a big insect, such as a dangerous wasp, out of the spider's web. Humans are one of the biggest dangers to daddy longlegs spiders. People kill spiders and clean up the daddy longlegs spiders' messy webs with brooms and vacuum cleaners.

Birds, lizards, wasps, and other spiders, including other daddy longlegs spiders, attack Pholcidae. This bird has used the messy web as part of her nest!

Daddy Longlegs Spiders and Humans

Some people think that daddy longlegs spiders are dangerous to people. This is not true. There is no record of one of these long-legged spiders ever having bitten a person. Some scientists believe that daddy longlegs spiders have such small, weak jaws that they couldn't bite a person if they wanted to. In fact, daddy longlegs spiders help people by eating harmful insects such as mosquitoes and cockroaches. They also eat pests that damage farmers' crops and kill dangerous spiders. So think twice before you clean up a messy spiderweb. You might be better off letting that daddy longlegs spider hang around your house!

Many spiders that live in people's houses die in the vacuum cleaner. If you want daddy longlegs to eat household pests, be careful when you vacuum!

Glossary

abdomen (AB-duh-min) The large, rear section of a spider's body.

arachnids (uh-RAK-nidz) Bugs that have two body parts and four pairs of legs.

breed (BREED) To make babies.

cephalothorax (seh-fuh-loh-THOR-aks) A spider's smaller, front body part, containing its head.

complicated (KOM-pluh-kayt-ed) Hard to understand or figure out.

glands (GLANDZ) Organs or a parts of the body that produce a substance to help with a bodily function.

paralyzes (PAR-uh-lyz-iz) Causes to lose feeling or movement in the limbs.

Pholcidae (FOHL-sih-day) The family of spiders to which daddy longlegs spiders belong.

prey (PRAY) Animals that are hunted by other animals for food.

species (SPEE-sheez) A single kind of plant or animal. All people are one species.

spinnerets (spih-nuh-RETS) Parts, located on the rear of the spider's abdomen, that release silk.

survive (sur-VYV) To stay alive.

transparent (tranz-PER-ent) Able to be seen through, sheer.

tropics (TRAH-piks) The warm parts of Earth.

unsuspecting (un-suh-SPEKT-ing) Unaware.

venom (VEH-num) A poison passed by one animal into another through a bite or a sting.

Index

Web Sites

Due to the changing nature of Internet links, PowerKids Press has developed an online list of Web sites related to the subject of this book. This site is updated regularly. Please use this link to access the list: www.powerkidslinks.com/lspi/dadlong/